EXPLORING MONTREAL'S
UNDERGROUND CITY

EXPLORING

Montreal's Underground

CITY

Alan Hustak

Véhicule Press
MONTRÉAL

Published with the generous assistance of the Canada Book Fund of the
Department of Canadian Heritage.

Funded by the
Government
of Canada | Canadä

Cover design: David Drummond
Page 2: Sculpture "Solstice" by Guido Molinari, in Simons department store
Maps by Yannick Allen-Larochelle
Typeset in Minion by Simon Garamond
Printed by Marquis Printing Inc.

LIBRARY AND ARCHIVES CANADA CATALOGUING IN PUBLICATION

Hustak, Alan, 1944-, author
Exploring Montreal's underground city / Alan Hustak.

Includes index.
Issued in print and electronic formats.
ISBN 978-1-55065-479-0 (softcover). – ISBN 978-1-55065-487-5
(epub)

1. Underground areas – Québec (Province) – Montréal –
Guidebooks.
2. Montréal (Québec) – Guidebooks. 3. Montréal (Québec) –
Description and travel. I. Title.

FC2947.18.H884 2017   917.14'28045   C2017-903143-0
C2017-903144-9

Distributed in Canada by LitDistCo
Distributed in the U.S. by Independent Publishers Group

Published by Véhicule Press, Montréal, Québec, Canada
vehiculepress.com

Printed in Canada on FSC certified paper.

Contents

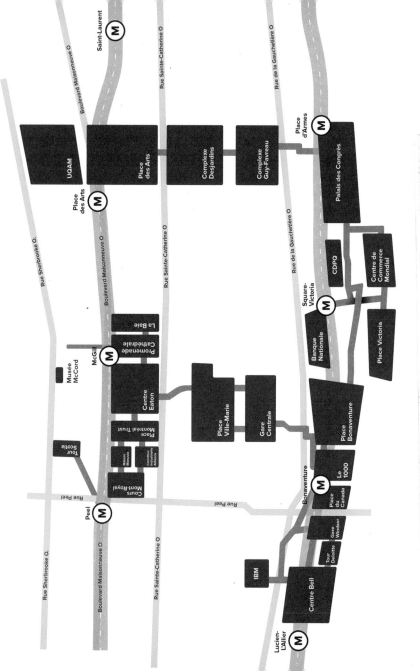

A City within a City

"Through a happy combination of expert foresight, private initiative, and luck, Montreal is about to become the first 21st century city in North America…what sets (it) apart is not so much its towers, but their spreading roots in a multilevel of shops, transportation systems, and pedestrian promenades…."

– Peter Blake, *Architectural Forum*, 1966

Let's skip the city streets and sidewalks for an afternoon, let's put on our walking shoes and ramble through Montreal's interior city—an underground multi-level city, a weather-protected system of walkways. We'll meander along its connecting passageways above and below the metropolis. No other city in the world has anything quite as distinct—a city enclosed with a city, a burrowed borough so vast that it houses no less than Almost Everything. Montreal's subterranean city was born during the same burst of civic ambition that gave rise to the Expo 67 World's Fair and exerts a reputation not shared by similar undertakings such as Toronto's PATH network or Calgary's Plus 15 system of enclosed overhead walkways.

Montreal architect Avi Friedman believes the underground city's renown is the result of a "perfect storm of events" that reshaped the city in the 1960s. "The Metro was being developed, Expo 67 was being built. Developers bought up large tracts of land which allowed their shopping malls to be connected to the Metro. All this all happened when people came to Expo and Montreal itself became famous. The underground city became prominent and became known around the world because many, many people wrote about it."

By their very nature cities evolve over time. Unlike the natural city which has grown above ground between the St. Lawrence River and Mount Royal during the last four centuries, Montreal is unique in that it also comprises this sprawling, artificial city, one which was deliberately created over the past half century by urban planners, developers, designers and landscape architects.

Since Place Ville Marie opened in 1962, the landmark skyscraper has been at the heart of a pedestrian network that grew into an extraordinary, enclosed shopper's paradise, where the climate is always ideal. This other, creative city has all the necessary ingredients that urbanist Jane Jacobs says constitute a great city:

- It serves more than one primary function.
- It is a mix of buildings that vary in age and condition.
- It harbours a dense concentration of people
- Finally, the blocks within this parallel city below ground are short.

It all began with an Italian-American urban designer with the aristocratic sounding name of Vincent de Pasciuto-Ponte who is rarely given credit for the concept. Montrealers in the early 60s weren't quite sure what to make of this slight, refined urban planner when he first arrived to work on Place Ville Marie. "His sleek elegance, combined with a certain sinister air, generated by the dark glasses he invariably wears, suggest a Mafioso," is the way the Montreal *Star's* Lou Seligson profiled him. Similarly, *Le Jour's* Evelyn Dumas referred to him as the man with a *visage buriné* "who dreamed in 3-D." *Time* magazine dubbed him "the Multi-level man." Ponte was born in Boston in 1919 into a wealthy immigrant family in 1919. He obtained a fine arts degree from Harvard in 1949. He won a Fullbright scholarship to study architecture in Rome but dropped out after his first term because he recognized other students in his class were better than he was. Not prepared to be "a second-rate architect," he became instead a first rate urban planner. Ponte studied with I.M. Pei, and when Pei's firm became involved in the Place Ville Marie project Ponte was chosen to

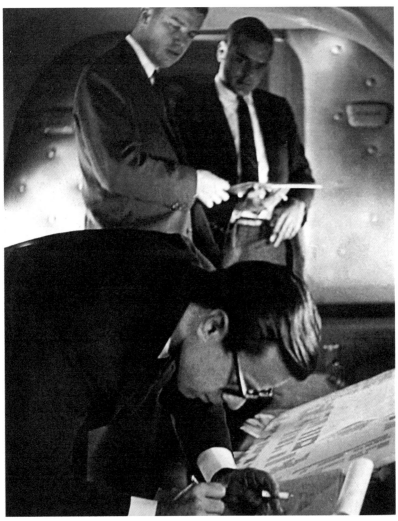

Urban designer Vincent Ponte (foreground) envisioned a new environment for his adopted city which he called "a multi-level, interconnected city."

help draw up the master plan. Ponte was so taken with Montreal he moved to the city from New York in 1964 saying that of all North American cities, only New York or San Francisco could rival Montreal.

Inspired by *Città Nuova*, a futurist concept first advanced in 1915 by influential architect Antonio Sant'Elia, Ponte envisioned a new environment for his adopted city which he called "a multi-level, interconnected city." Ponte advocated the notion of a sheltered city, "the most advanced, comprehensive, and successful instance of downtown planning in the world—a true multi-level centre—clusters of office towers and other buildings rise from a common base structure composed of plazas, malls, covered shopping areas, underground trucking networks, and parking garages, all of these elements inter-woven and interconnected, linking the separate buildings together by their common roots." In short, the idea, in his words, was to reduce downtown traffic and "preserve mobility in the midst of highest densities." To do this, he argued, development must be compressed and built upwards, downwards and sideways to serve a variety of purposes. Listening to Ponte explain his theories was, according to one realtor, similar to attending an Elvis Costello concert, "horned rimmed glasses, a shock of black hair, and a hypnotic sound."

His original concept was to turn McGill College Avenue into a cere-monial boulevard with identical buildings on both sides much like the Rue de Rivoli in Paris. Beneath the boulevard, between the Queen Elizabeth Hotel on René Levesque Boulevard and McGill's Roddick Gates on Sherbrooke Street would be a vast underground gallery and shopping mall. "A physical structure in the downtown area that could appropriately contain and heighten life and movement, and serve the city as the physical symbol of its self image." Critics, however, rejected the formal plan because they suggested Ponte's scheme was "an aerial example of a beaux-arts layout", that was out of keeping with "the informal cluster of towers which give Montreal its dynamic character."

His visionary plan for a new downtown environment proved to be a hard sell.

Montreal in the late 1950s was not the cosmopolitan place it is today. City planners scoffed at the suggestion that private developers would pay extra to plug their buildings into such a network or that pedestrians would want make use of the tunnels. A number of merchandising experts were dead set against the idea, arguing that people would not "shop in a basement." Ponte ignored them "Build it," he seems to have reasoned, "and they will come." He was right. In other words, if thought and energy, form and function, go into a project, the likelihood that it will succeed increases.

Place Ville Marie was the first project to trigger the whole enterprise. From the day it opened in the heart of the city it was wildly popular. Ponte also seems to have rightly envisioned the Metro, Montreal's long-awaited subway system, as the real spine and bloodstream of his underground city, and to have seen that the below ground city spreads naturally from the existence of a more family city thing: the below grade train.

The multidimensional city depends on a subway system to serve as its nervous system, and a series of tunnels and walkways to function as its connective tissue. Montreal's underground city was midwife to a remarkable rebirth of the whole downtown core. On the whole, a kind of virtuous circle begins that Ponte anticipated—when people are brought in below ground they are eager to come up above ground. As he explained it, "You create a permeable membrane between the underworld and the overworld, all based on foot traffic—on the pedestrians, the walkers, who are the city's red blood cells without whom a city pales and sickens and dies of anemia."

As early as 1967, when the world came to Montreal for the World's Fair, the concept of an underground network captured international attention. In a ten-page spread, entitled *Multi Level City: Towards a New Environment in Downtown Montreal,* The prestigious *Architectural Review* described Montreal as "the most dynamically growing downtown area… a model that other cities are well to study. That it has achieved a pre-eminent position is to some extent due to business enterprise and foresight, and also, it must be said, to a series of accidents. The first of these was the large area of downtown Montreal (amounting to 22 acres) in possession of one owner, Canadian National Railways, whose president, Donald Gordon, saw the opportunities it presented." Gordon won the support of the city's dynamic Mayor Jean Drapeau. And as the *New Yorker*'s essayist Adam Gopnick pointed out in a 2011 Massey Lecture, "Two simple changes (and who exactly spurred them is a matter of some debate) helped and were hugely important. One assured that everything in the city below a certain point, would be public property. In Montreal, somewhat uniquely, you have a complicated lease arrangement where everything below ground is common property which belongs to everybody. You can tunnel by right, if not quite at will."

Landscape architects often refer to design elements as "moves," as if they were engaged in a game of chess. Those who are most successful follow a strategy that involves a series of small moves, rather than one big one. Move by calculated move, Ponte took his cues from the buildings that were already there and anticipated those that were to come.

Ponte figured out the balance.

Since its inception over five decades ago, La Ville Souterraine, the Underground City has grown into a parallel metropolis, an amazing labyrinth of burrowed passageways, wide hallways, alleys, and atriums that snake their way along over 32 kilometres (20 miles), to connect 80 downtown skyscrapers, ten major hotels, 2,000 stores, apartment blocks, and even a wax museum. All of it linked to the city's 68 Metro stations.

A tour of the Underground City can be both a delightful surprise and a disappointment—a surprise because it is so eyepoppingly big, so convenient; a disappointment, because ultimately, in reality, it is little more than one vast shopping mall.

People are drawn to it because it is weatherproof and because they can move through it easily. The reward is see how many disparate environments blend into a unified whole.

There are 120 entrances along its route, through Metro stations, office towers and department stores, so it's easy to access and create your own path. You can walk between buildings in minutes. Travel through the pertinent sections and decide for yourself if it is a delight or a disappointment.

Like the city above ground the underground city has its own mix of sun and shade, public squares, fountains, green spaces, gardens and even an indoor skating rink. It is not so much an underground city—that's a misnomer—as it is an enclosed, weatherproof city: a climate-controlled environment, above and below ground that is air-conditioned in summer and warm against the blast of winter. It is properly called a RESO, which is not an acronym, but rather a homonym, a play on the French word, *Reseau* which means Network. City planners and developers from around the world still come to Montreal to pay homage to Ponte, (there is memorial to him on the esplanade of Place Ville Marie, overlooking McGill College Avenue) and to study the RESO, which has served as the prototype for similar ventures in Toronto, Halifax and Calgary.

Design critic Emmanuelle Viera describes Montreal's underground network as "incoherent, imperfect, but it holds its own. It is the image of its own society: lively, diverse and creative, linked intimately with the culture of consumption." Detractors like author and travel writer Taras Grescoe see it as a cross between a shopping mall and a bomb shelter, "an overheated bunker, a Mall of the Americas on the moon. An afternoon in its concrete entrails leaves you feeling that a revival of Inuit igloos and habitant farmhouses might not be such a bad idea."

Heritage Montreal's Dinu Bumbaru, however, says the notion that the underground city is one big shopping mall is a misconception. "The personality of one big shopping centre is reductive. It is much more than a functional set of cubes, You have large and distinctive spaces like the atrium at Complexe Desjardins and Central Station which serve public functions, the scale of the enclosed civic spaces is enormous. The underground city doesn't only serve retail functions but incorporates civic venues as well."

Someone living in an apartment block above the network can avail themselves of everything they need without ever having to go outdoors. The pathways that unite the various components embrace the anarchy of the city and link the various residential, retail and cultural cores creating a fluid, highly livable and vibrant underground urban opus. In 2006 a 5 km marathon race was held throughout the passageways as part of Montréal en Lumière (the Winter Festival of Lights), starting at the Peel Metro station and ending at Complexe Desjardins. Organizer Michel Labreque explained that the marathon—with 486 steps to climb and 569 to descend—was designed as a tourist attraction that would enable "people to navigate the course as a sight-seeing excursion and for exercise." It looked as if it might become an annual event, but it never has.

Unlike similar pathways in other cities, there are no connecting sky links above ground; both Ponte and Montreal's autocratic Mayor Jean Drapeau regarded them as an unsightly blight on the streetscape.

It is far from perfect, but as Fabien Deglise writes in *Montreal Souterrain, sous le beton, le myth*: "It is a trip to explore the various disjointed compontents, a surreal marriage of public and commercial spaces, theatres, art galleries, public transit, a hospital and the headquarters for international agencies as well as centres of high finance."

Each year, during Montreal's Nuit Blanche, during the winter Montréal en Lumière festival in mid-February, the system becomes a temporary art gallery—Art Souterrain—when the works of more than 80 contemporary artists are on display.

The underground system is a confusing place to navigate, even for people who are familiar with it. But it is marked with maps, pictograms and overhead signs. This guide will help you navigate the whole network, and introduce readers to its many joys and byways.

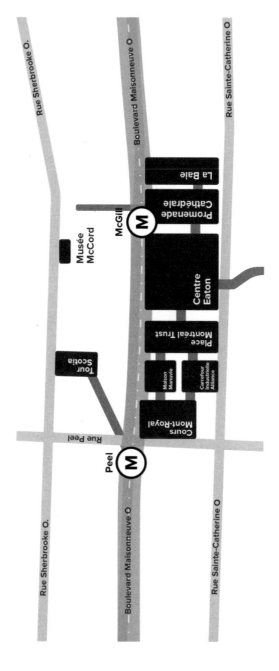

16

The Downtown Core

The entirety of the subterranean system was the result of conscious decisions envisioned and executed by a generation of urbanists who, for once, got it mostly right, and they have gone on, getting it right ever since…."

– Adam Gopnick, *Winter: Five Windows on the Season*

Tour Scotia (Scotia Tower)

To tour the main downtown section of the underground city it is probably easiest to begin at the Scotia Tower (1002 Sherbrooke Street W.) across from McGill University, one of the RESO,'s entry points which leads to the Peel Metro station, and then into Les Cours Mont-Royal. The 27-storey bank tower opened in 1990 and remains a singularly unattractive building on the city skyline. Take a look at the paintings by Montreal artist Jean McEwen, (1923-1999) which are a triptych entitled *En remontant les rouges* (Raising the Reds) installed in the mezzanine high up on your left above the banking floor. The colour, brushwork and fluttering tension of the panels have a disembodying effect. McEwan is considered to be one of Canada's most influential abstract painters. Unless you are looking to buy gold, there isn't much else to see. Walk through the bank into the lobby and take the escalators to your left down through a utilitarian passageway to the Metro level.

Peel Metro Station

Head into the Peel Metro station and follow the signs for Les Cours Mont-Royal. The Peel Metro is decorated with a play of 37 ceramic circles which represent movement. (Originally there were 54. but 17 were removed during renovations to the station. They are the work of artist Jean-Paul Mousseau (1927-1991). He was among the first artists in Quebec to see the necessity of integrating public art into the urban environment. When the metro was under construction, the city's Mayor Jean Drapeau decreed that the various stations be decorated with figurative works which represented scenes from Montreal's history. The Peel station, for example, is named for British Prime Minister Sir Robert Peel, who lifted Imperial economic control of Britain's trade with its colonies which led to Montreal's economic growth in the 1850s. Rather than commission Mousseau to incorporate a likeness of a British statesman in an important downtown station, Drapeau gave Mousseau free reign to work with the architects of the metro station to come up with the non-figurative circles. Six of them are 6 metres in diameter, the other 31 two metres in diameter.

Peel Metro station

Les Cours Mont-Royal

The Peel Metro station opens into Les Cours Mont-Royal (1455 Peel Street), a one-stop fashion mall. The building you are in began life in 1922 as the 1,100-room Sheraton Mount Royal Hotel. When the hotel opened, it was the largest of its kind in the British Empire. Its Normandie Roof club—the Montreal version of New York's Rainbow room in Rockefeller Center—was a fashionable supper club that featured headliners like Frank Sinatra, and live radio broadcasts of dance music. The hotel was gutted in 1987 and its suites were converted into high-end condominium apartments.

As you enter the atrium on the Metro level (Niveau Métro), hanging below the skylight are six birdmen sculptures by Inuit Artist David Ruben Piqtoukun (1950-) who hails from from Paulatuk, Northwest Territories. They are called *Tingmiluks* and represent shamans or shape shifters who are able to transform themselves into winged creatures carried aloft by the wind spirit, Sila. Beneath the hotel's original vaulted turquoise and gold ceiling, to your right, is a 200-bulb glass chandelier that once graced the Mount Royal Hotel main lobby; it is said to have been imported from a casino in Monte Carlo.

The Cours Mont-Royal shopping court has four levels of shops, most of them clothing stores including the recently expanded Harry Rosen, DKNY, Sarah Pacini, and Matinique. You'll also find an Ethan Allen furniture outlet tucked away on the third floor. One of the more intriguing attractions up the first flight of stairs under the atrium is the largest permanent haute couture Barbie Expo, a museum which has more than one thousand dolls on display. Admission is free.

PHOTOS
1 David Ruben Piqtoukun's *Tingmiluks*
2 The Barbie Museum

Carrefour Industrielle Alliance Building

Return down the stairs to the Metro level. Walking toward the escalator ahead of you, take the corridor to the left past Starbucks into the Carrefour Industrielle Alliance Building (977 Sainte-Catherine W.), which once housed a retail department store known as Murphy's and later the Robert Simpson Co. Ltd. Simpson's moved there in 1929, remodeled the building and remained at the location for the next 60 years. The insurance company that bought the building in 1989 converted it into a retail complex which today houses the Montreal flagship of the Simons department store chain and the Scotiabank Cinema complex with 12 screens including an IMAX experience.

Simons Department Store

The food court in the building, L'Espace Restaurants, is the first of many you will find in the underground city. Instead of stopping for a snack, ride the escalators in the middle of the court up to the Simons store. It is worth going up even if only to see Montreal-born artist Guido Molinari's 25-foot-high clear, geometric modular sculpture, *Solstice*, which hangs above the escalators. *(See p. 2).* The sculpture melds colours associated with the four seasons, dark saturated shades for winter, and warm bright tints representing autumn, spring and summer. Molinari (1933-2004) was an inventive abstract painter and sculptor who believed that colour didn't exist by itself, and only exists in shape and dimension and in its correlation with other colours. Simons is a high-quality, but reasonably-priced chain of stores that had its beginnings in 1840 when John Simon opened a dry goods store in Quebec City. It is still family owned.

Maison Manuvie

The latest addition to the network, is a sleek 27-storey office tower at 900 de Maisonneuve Boulevard. designed by Menkès Shooner Dagenais Letourneux. It plugged into the network in November, 2017. The lobby has a wall featuring 500 constantly changing panels of colour, a creation known as the *Colorimeter* designed by electronic artist Rafael Lozano-Hemmer (who was born in Mexico and graduated from Montreal's Concordia University).

1 Cours Mont-Royal
2 Olly Fresco's prepared food and buffet emporium in 2 locations:
Promenades Cathédrale (pictured) and Carrefour Industrielle Alliance Building

Bell Media Centre | Place Montreal Trust

Returning to the Metro level (Niveau Métro) beneath Simons, turning right takes you to the Bell Media Centre (1800 McGill College), a 30-storey postmodern skyscraper which houses Montreal Trust (1500 McGill College). The shopping concourse opened in 1988 and houses Zara, the exclusive Spanish clothing chain that doesn't believe in advertising, and Indigo Books, Montreal and Canada's largest bookstore chain. Downstairs are Winner's and a Dollarama discount outlet. The building is connected to a sleek 27-storey office tower (900 de Maisonneuve) designed by Menkès Shooner Dagenais and LeTourneux between Cours Mont Royal and the Manulife Centre. It was the latest building to be plugged into the network in November, 2017.

As you circle the metro level of Place Montreal Trust you will see a huge fountain spurting orgasmic jets of water. *(Photo opp. page)* It is one of two such water jet fountains in the underground city, (the other one is in Complex Desjardins) and it is thought to be among the tallest indoor fountains in North America. This fountain is 20 metres high, and every five minutes or so it spurts water 30 metres higher. Each December, during the holiday season the fountain is converted into a huge, indoor Christmas tree decorated with oversized ornaments.

On the other side of the fountain, beside the Info Booth (beside another Starbucks) you'll see Robin Bell's *The Goalie*. A cast bronze 400-kilogram scupture of Ken Dryden, the legendary Montreal Canadiens goalie and lawyer who went on to become a Liberal Member of Parliament and a cabinet minister in Prime Minister Jean Chretien's government.

PHOTOS
1 Place Montreal Trust entrance
2 Place Montreal Trust's large indoor fountain

Centre Eaton (Eaton Centre) and McGill Metro

Opposite the Info Booth is the passageway that will take you to the Eaton Centre (705 Sainte-Catherine W.). After 130 years in business the iconic T. Eaton Company which had a chain of department stores went bankrupt in 1999 and closed its doors. It once controlled 60 per cent of all department store sales in Canada. The Eaton Centre houses the Grévin wax museum hall on the top floor (Level 5). It's very similar to the one in Paris, and showcases more than 120 life-size figures arranged in lavish settings including President Barack Obama, Katy Perry, Einstein, Michael Jackson, Elvis Presley, Sydney Crosby, Charles Aznavour, Justin Bieber, Justin Trudeau, and Quebec celebrities such as Céline Dion, Diane Dufresne, Jean-Pierre Ferland, Robert Charlebois and Luc Plamondon.

Straight ahead to your left, at the north end of the Eaton Centre you can access the McGill Metro station and two office towers, 2020 University and Place London Life. The metro features 5 painted glass murals, *La vie à Montréal au XIXe siècle* by Nicolas Sollogoub. The first two mayors of Montreal, Peter McGill (1759-1860) and Jacques Viger (1787-1858) are depicted. (Peter McGill was not related to James McGill, the founder of the nearby university which bears his name.)

The Eaton Centre is connected to Complexe Les Ailes (677 Sainte-Catherine W.), a shopping concourse built when the former Eaton department store was gutted in 2002. The former restaurant on the ninth floor (now closed to the public) remains an architectural gem. Imagine if you will an elegantly proportioned art deco room inspired by transatlantic French luxury liners of the 1920s, or by the Palais Trocadéro and the Palais de Chaillot in Paris. The matriarch of the family, Lady Flora McCrea Eaton, a member of the company's board of directors, commissioned the acclaimed interior designer Jacques Carlu (1890-1976) to design additions to the stores in Montreal and Toronto. According to *Lunch with Lady Eaton*, The Montreal dining room was inspired by the luxury liner, *Ile de France*, and its design reflected the elongated formality of the ship's first-class dining room. Carlu taught advanced design at the Massachusetts Institute of Technology and was also responsible for the Rainbow Room in New York's Rockefeller Plaza. The restaurant in the Montreal Eaton's opened in 1931. It is perfectly proportioned, 40 metres long and 23 metres wide with a ceiling 14 metres high. On either side are two smaller dining rooms, the Gold and Silver rooms. At either end of the main room are two allegorical cubist murals painted by Carlu's wife, Natasha, *Pleasure of the Chase* and *Pleasures of Peace*. After Eaton's went bankrupt, the flagship store was sold to Ivanhoé-Cambridge, a real estate arm of the Caisse de dépôt et placement du Québec, which invests funds from the Quebec pension plan. Even though the 9th floor has been declared a heritage site by the provincial government, it is off limits to the public and the classification does not oblige the owner to maintain or conserve the space.

If you need to stock up on wine and liquor, the SAQ (Société des alcools du Québec) can be found on the Metro level.

Centre Eaton.

Promenades Cathédrale

From the Metro level of the Eaton Centre turn right at the SAQ and follow signs to the Proménades Cathédrale (625 Sainte-Catherine W.), so-called because the shopping mall was once the crypt of Christ Church Anglican Cathedral which is directly above ground. Take the escalators on your right to Sainte-Catherine Street. Immediately to your left is the Cathedral's main entrace.To give you an idea of the engineering ingenuity that went into building this portion of the underground city the century-old Neo-gothic cathedral was held aloft on stilts when foundations to build the shopping mall were laid. The Cathedral was built in 1859 by Montreal's first Anglican bishop, Francis Fulford, and is similar to the Anglican cathedral in Fredericton, New Brunswick, which was designed by the same architect, Frank Wills. Both are patterned after a church in Norfolk, England. Worth a peek are the windows from the William Morris studio in London, the ornamental screen above the altar, memorial plaques, and the children's chapel. The painting of *The Last Supper* to the right of the high altar was saved from the fire in 1856 that razed the first Christ Church Anglican Cathedral.

La Baie (The Bay) Department Store

Return the way you came back to Metro level. Proceed right to The Bay (585 Sainte-Catherine W.), the last of the city's big downtown department stores. It opened as Morgan's in 1890 and the store stands on a site that was home to the wife and children of U.S. Confederate president Jefferson Davis, whose family lived in Montreal during the Civil War. A plaque in French on the east side of the building marked the location until it was removed in August, 2017. It's an enormous store built of imported red Scottish sandstone that gleams in commercial and historic splendor. Some of its foundations are stones taken from the United Canada's first Parliament Building, which burned in 1849. Morgan's was bought in 1960 by the Hudson Bay Company the oldest North American Corporate entity, having been founded in 1670. Then in 2008 The Bay was acquired by NRDC Equity, which also owns Lord & Taylor, the oldest upscale retail department store chain in the United States. The Bay is being renovated to accommodate a Saks Fifth Avenue OFF 5th location. The Bay acquired Saks, a high-end luxury goods store in 2013, and has opened outlets across Canada. There aren't many upscale shops like Saks within the underground city. High end merchandise and underground tunnels generally do not go hand in hand. A survey done by Université de Montréal urbanists Gerard Beaudet and Paul Lewis found that 80 per cent of the shops and boutiques in the network offer discount or inexpensive merchandise, 20 per cent more than the number of downtown stores at street level.

If you wish, Place Ville Marie can be accessed from the Tunnel level of the Eaton Centre.

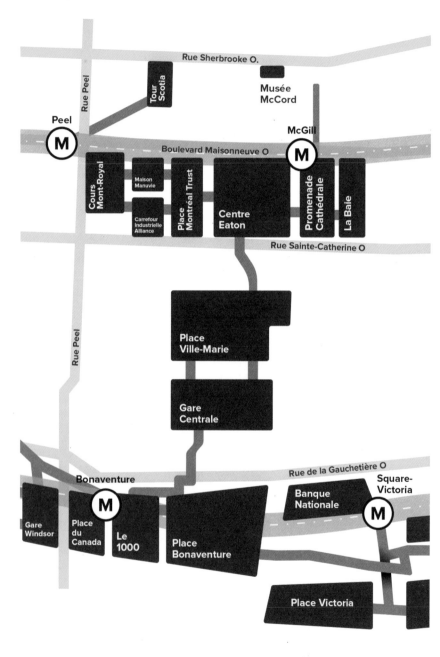

Place Ville Marie—Where it All Began

"*The defining character of the underground city is the high fluidity of the traffic. People are drawn to it in the first place because they can move around easily. There are no cars, no trucks, not even any bicycles. …the underground appeared first and grew fastest in Montreal for several reasons unique to that city: Punishing weather, an excellent subway system, a commitment to the tourist industry, and a large downtown residential community.*"

– Fred Hapgood, writing in *Attaché*, March 1998

With the opening in 1993 of the tunnel beneath Sainte-Catherine Street which connects the Eaton Centre with Place Ville Marie (PVM), a major link in the development of the multi-level city centre was completed. Place Ville Marie (1 Place Ville Marie), at the heart of the downtown core, was at last connected to five shopping malls in the main east-west corridor that stretches seven city blocks from Peel Street to Phillips Square. During the 1980s the underground city spread its tentacles as mid-town developers built eight new towers, all of them plugged into the pedestrian system. Instead of cramped, snakey tunnels, many of the new buildings incorporated atriums, plazas, courts and arcades, and areas known as "spacefalls." It became a new urban experience, intensified, concentrated and purified. The hallways that connected Place Ville Marie's 80 stores and boutiques, which had been the nucleus of the system, now mushroomed in all directions. There were now as many boutiques below ground as there were above. The system became even more sophisticated and so attractive to shoppers that civic planners were concerned that any further expansion of the understreet network would suck the life from the surface and siphon customers away from other skyscrapers and stores that were not part of the system. The situation was further complicated by a revolution in the retail business and the dramatic rise of big box stores in the suburbs which drained shoppers away from the downtown core and contributed to the failure of two major department stores, Eaton and Simpson. Writing in *La Presse,* urbanist Christophe Caron complained that is was "criminal to spend fortunes building basements, leaving nothing to develop the vacant lots above ground." Architect Peter Sijpkes similary warned that it would be "a tragedy if the gloss below street level came at the price of grime and crime above."

As a result, Mayor Jean Doré's administration declared a moratorium on further expansion of the underground network. It would remain incomplete for another fifteen years.

Because Montreal is built on the slope of a modest mountain, the so-called underground city is really stepped into the side of it. You walk

With its cross-shaped tower, Place Ville Marie is a Montreal landmark.

directly into Place Ville Marie from Cathcart Street, then go down a full flight of steps to Central Station which is at street level with La Gauchetière and then some steps further down into Place Bonaventure which takes you further down on St. Jacques. Originally, there was to be a pedestrian skywalk across La Gauchetière linking Place Bonaventure with Central Station but Mayor Drapeau thought overhead skywalks were unslightly and killed the idea.

To access Place Ville Marie from the Eaton Centre go to the basement level (Niveau Tunnel one floor below the Metro level), walk through the corridor past foreign exchange marts, discount clothing stores, drycleaners and travel agencies, until you reach the second set of escalators which carry you into Place Ville Marie's 285,000 square-metre retail shopping plaza which equals the space of the 47-storey skyscraper above it. It was the first major project to bring the traditional outdoor marketplace in from the cold and it paved the way for a renaissance of urban development in Montreal.

"Although the shops have for the most part no rear access (deliveries have to be made from the public promenades in the early morning or late at night) they have been highly successful commercially, this is no doubt partly due to the comfortable shopping conditions, especially in winter, but far more important, in their integration into the transportation system."

The Observatory's 360°-view of the city on the 46th floor and the 4-seasons terrace on the 44th floor is unparalleled. An exhibition on the top floor offers an "immersive experience," featuring touch screens that highlight the best of Montreal. (Ticket prices: http://www.ausommetpvm.com/en/) The Les Enfants Terrible brasserie on the 44th floor, despite the view, is less than satisfactory. The waiting time is long and it does not accept reservations for groups smaller than six. An admission fee is not required to access the restaurant.

Fairmount Queen Elizabeth Hotel

From Place Ville Marie follow signs for the Gare Centrale and Bonaventure and head through the second set of glass doors that take you to the newly-renovated Fairmont Queen Elizabeth Hotel, the first of six luxury hotels connected to the network. The 1,200-room, 21-story hotel opened in 1958 and was the first air-conditioned hotel in North America and the first with direct dial telephones in each room. Cuban revolutionary leader Fidel Castro was the first guest to sign the register but perhaps the hotel's most celebrated guests were John Lennon and Yoko Ono who wrote the anthem *Give Peace a Chance* in a suite on the 17th floor during their 1969 Bed-in. Built by Canadian National Railways, the hotel was the keystone of the major renewal of Montreal's downtown core. It is built on 160 concrete pylons that help cushion the vibrations of the trains that rumble beneath it. A passageway connecting the hotel to the concourse of Central Station was the first indication of the network that was to come.

The hotel's reception lobby is longer than a regulation football field. Just off the lobby is the Marché Artisans—a grand urban market with artisanal products from Quebec and around the world, plus an extensive seafood bar.

PHOTOS
1 Suite where John Lennon and Yoko Ono spent their now-famous
  "bed-in for peace"
2 The hotel's lobby

36

Gare Centrale (Central Station)

From the lobby of the Queen Elizabeth Hotel return the way you came through the glass doors and take the escalators to descend into Montreal's Central Station, Central Station's concourse is the underground city's first outpost, its main public square. Designed by architect John Campbell Merrett, it opened in 1943 as Canadian National Railway's depot. Three storeys tall, 350 feet long and 104 feet wide, it has a curious intimacy in spite of its dimensions. It has been estimated that more than 50,000 people walk through the station each day. The monumental friezes at either end of the concourse celebrate Canada's national anthem. It is the work of Charles Comfort (1900-1994) and the bas reliefs were executed in the 1950s by stone carver Sebastiano Aiello, before Comfort went on to become director of the National Gallery of Canada in Ottawa. The east wall depicts our fundamental freedoms, and the west wall is a salute to our natural resources. It incorporates a number of playful elements, like the boy with the slingshot, and a tiny gopher in the shade of a huge Prairie grain elevator. His intention, Comfort said, was "to depict the daily life of Canadians, their hopes, and to some extent to show their environment." Comfort signed the mural with a self-portrait. You can find it among the bas reliefs on the southwest corner, just above the words "Patriot Love." If you take the time to read carefully you will find a mistake in the words of the anthem, which should be "We stand on guard for thee." Words have been transposed, and instead it reads "Stand we on guard for thee." At the west end of the station are Les Halles de la Gare, a network of boutiques and places to eat. The popular Première Moisson is the ideal spot to pick up pastries, patés, bread and sandwiches. The food court has a number of relatively quiet alcoves where you can sit and catch your breath. To purchase wine and spirits there is an SAQ outlet.

Return to Comfort's "South" mural in the corner of the vast hall, and enter the convoluted passageway (direction Place Bonaventure) until you reach the end. Then take the escalators on your right down to the lower level.

PHOTOS
1 Frieze in Central Station by Charles Comfort
2 Les Halles de la Gare—shopping and places to eat

Le 1000 de la Gauchetière

Should you continue straight ahead into Place Bonaventure, skip to page 44. However, you can veer to the right and head for Montreal's tallest skyscraper, Le 1000 de la Gauchetière. At 205 metres, the Postmodern building designed by Lemay & Associates and Dimakopoulos and Associates is a copy of the JP Morgan Chase Tower in Dallas, Texas. The building is situated above a busy transit hub, and it also has an indoor iceskating rink (Patinoire atrium) where you can rent skates and execute figure 8s year round. Don't miss going upstairs to the mezzanine see the laser clock, then turn around to the large curved window which perfectly frames the dome of Mary Queen of the World Cathedral, seat of Montreal's Roman Catholic archdiocese. To the right of the information desk on the mezannine is a wall honouring the great builders of Montreal's economy, including entreprenurs Paul Desmarais and Stephen Jarislowsky.

Marriott Château Champlain

Return to the Metro level and proceed to the Bonaventure Metro Station and walk towards Gare Lucien-L'Allier. At the end of the station turn left and follow signs to the Marriott Château Champlain, known as the "cheese grater" hotel because of the half-moon windows on each of its 36 floors. The hotel is such a familiar Montreal landmark it is hard to believe that it has only been around since Expo 67—the World's Fair. Designed by Montreal architects D'Astous & Pothier, it was built as a Canadian Pacific Railway Hotel, and sold to the Marriott Chain in 1995. D'Astous was one of Frank Lloyd Wright's students, and the arched windows are believed to have been inspired by The Marin County Civic Centre which was Wright's last commission. The Bonaventure Metro station beneath the hotel has walkways that branch into the 1250 René-Lévesque Building and the Bell Centre to the west and to Place Bonaventure to the east. From the hotel you can take the elevator to the Bonaventure Metro level and head west into Windsor Station.

41

Tour Deloitte (Deloitte Tower) | Gare Windsor (Windsor Station) | Centre Bell

Connected to Windsor Station is the Deloitte Tower (1115 Saint-Antoine W.), a striking 26 storey-tower designed by the New York architectural firm, Kohn Pedersen Fox. The building which opened in 2015 has won awards for its strategic urban integration and its unique concept which integrates modern and heritage elements. Within the integrated Windsor Station complex next door is the Bell Centre (1909 Avenue des Canadiens-de-Montréal), home to the Montreal Canadiens and the city's shrine to hockey. When the arena opened in 1996 it replaced the Montreal Forum. There is a celebratory sense about the building. It covers almost four acres, and each of the 21,300 upholstered seats commands a sweeping view of the playing surface. It also has four restaurants, the most popular being La Cage aux Sports. Adjacent to the Bell centre is the 50-storey Tour des Canadiens, the city's second-tallest apartment building. Designed by Cardinal Hardy, Martin Marcotte, Beinhake, the tower has 520 condominiums.

A spur from the Bell Centre connects with the **1250 René-Lévesque Building**, an art deco, classic skyscraper that has been part of the city skyline since 1992 when it was known as the IBM Building. Initially jointly owned by Canadian Pacific and IBM, the $280-million, 50-storey tower with its sophisticated curved façade, was, like the Deliotte tower, designed by William Pedersen, a partner in the firm Kohn Pedersen Fox. The building occupies 151,900 square metres (1.6-million square feet). The changes of level and scale in the design complement the surrounding buildings without overpowering them and the black granite pergola at street level adds a measure of art-deco sophistication. The Decca 77 restaurant on the ground floor offers both fine dining and expensive bistro fare in an upscale atmosphere,

PHOTOS
1 Lobby of Deloitte Tower
2 Lobby of 1250 René-Lévesque Building

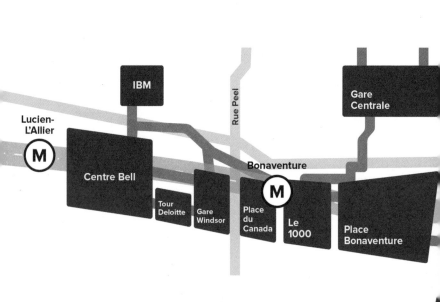

Place Bonaventure and the Quartier international

People like the sheltered city concept. They enjoy not having to walk in the rain or to trudge through cold and snow in mid-winter to shop. They like the idea of being able to go directly from their offices to a restaurant and do some shopping without ever putting on a coat….

– *Montreal at the Crossroads*, Donna Gabeline, Dane Lanken and Gordon Pape

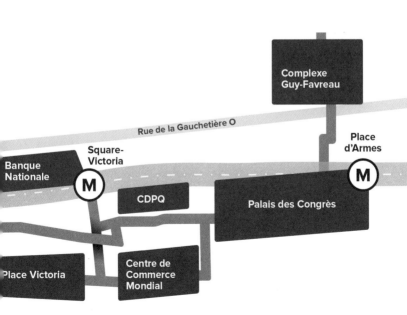

Place Bonaventure

Place Bonaventure (800 de la Gauchetière) is one of the world's largest indoor trade marts. It covers six acres and contains 3.2-million square feet of office space. Only Chicago's Merchandise Mart, at 4-million square feet is bigger. Montreal's convention centre and a concert hall were originally planned for the site, but those plans had to be abandoned when the Second World War began. It took another 25 years before the exhibition centre and trade mart opened, Designed by Raymond Affleck and his firm, the building made use of a highly textured concrete corduroy surface. He proclaimed: "What Italy can do with marble and stone, we can do with wood and concrete." When it opened in the spring of 1967 it was a brutal bunker without windows. The shopping arcades were largely gutted in 2002 when the building was given a $60-million facelift to make the building more inviting. The building is the site of the annual *Salon du Livres*, the immense and popular French-language bookfair, and an annual arts and craft gift show. Unless you are there for a trade show, there isn't all that much to see in the building. Known as the "Penthouse Hotel," the recently renovated 395-room luxury Hilton Hotel Bonaventure however, has a year-round outdoor rooftop swimming pool and sublime rooftop Japanese gardens. Leonardo DiCaprio was a guest in one of its suites during the filming of *The Aviator.*

International Civil Aviation Organization (ICAO)

Follow the directional signs to the south east corner of the building, go down a flight of stairs until you reach the tunnel that leads to the International Civil Aviation Organization tower. The United Nations agency has been in Montreal since 1945. It moved into its new headquarters (999 Robert-Bourassa) in 1996, a 17-storey building designed by Montreal architect Ken London. It is a formal and serious space with cherrywood panelling and aluminum acoustic ceilings. The history of civil aviation is told in a small museum on the ground floor which opened to commemorate the 70th anniversary of the 1944 Chicago Convention which created the international agency that governs international air transportation. Tours of the building can be arranged by appointment.

1 The Hotel Bonaventure's year-round outdoor rooftop swimming pool
2 The Montreal Canadiens promote the hockey team in the passageway leading
to the Bell Centre.

Quartier international (International Quarter)

Pick up the pace as you head through the emptiest stretch of the underground which runs through the International Quarter, a business district created in 1997 to bridge the downtown commerical core with Old Montreal. Anchored by the Civil Aviation Tower, the 27-hectare neighbourhood includes high-tech companies, offices for merchant shipping lines, customs brokers and banks that specialize in foreign investment. For the moment, the tunnel to the World Trade Centre is a nowhere zone, the only underdeveloped swatch of turf in the underground, a cream-walled, flourescent lit hallway with no stores, no ads, no buskers, no food courts, no Muzak and few people.

You might find the occasional homeless person curled up asleep in the passageway but there is nothing to fear as you walk through the multi-level city. Considering its size it is virtually crime free. Jean-Claude Marsan, the former director of the School of Architecture at the Université de Montréal insists it is "solid and safe" precisely because the corridors are always animated, "If you were to ask an urban planner today to duplicate the system, they wouldn't be able to do it. It grew organically, one day at a time."

It is estimated than on average 500,000 people use the walkways each day—even more in winter. As Adam Gopnick reminds us in *Winter: Five Windows on the Season*, "the possibility of walking below, in comfort, gives the city back to the walker whose natural mode is curiosity. Density tends to produce and reproduce density." In other words, there *is* safety in numbers.

"There is nothing new about indoor spaces in Montreal," maintains Heritage Montreal's Dinu Bumbaru. "Montreal had the Crystal Palace in the 19th century, there were underground tunnels in Chinatown, and both the Dominion Square Building and the Sun Life Building originally enclosed retail and commercial spaces. What has changed is the scale."

The constant stream of pedestrian traffic through the commercial areas adds to the delight of Montreal's urban experience. Almost all the corporate towers plugged into the network have their own security and security cameras to monitor the flow of pedestrian traffic. No one has ever been murdered in the underground city; the few arrests there are are for shoplifting, loitering or pickpocketing. Statistically, at least, it is safer to walk through the underground city than on the streets outdoors. The most recent figures suggest the crime rate outdoors is 2.93 for every 100,000 people; below ground it's 1.8.

Each year, during the first two weeks of March, the multi-level city is host to an artswalk, Art Souterrain, when the underground passageways areas are abuzz with more than a hundred art exhibitions, ineractive installations and performance art. The brainchild of its curator, Frédéric Loury, the annual event is part of the annual Montreal en Lumière winter festival and it is aimed at expanding the public`s appreciation of contemporary art. The show has become so successful that in 2010 it was awarded the Destination Centre-Ville prize as the best tourist draw in the city.

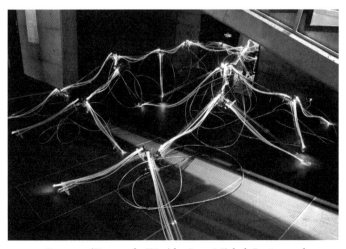

Quasar 3 (Danger du Zéro) by Jean-Michel Crettaz and
Mark-David Hosale, Art Souterrain, World Trade Centre

Édifice Jacques-Parizeau (Jaques Parizeau Building)

At the end of the long hall you will arrive at a web of four passageways that spin off in four directions. The tunnel directly ahead of you leads into to the Jacques Parizeau Building named for the former Quebec premier and finance minister (1930-2015). To the right is the route to the Stock Exchange Tower. Turn left and you will be walking towards the Place Victoria Metro station, the Bell Head Office and the sleek 35 storey Anima/Altoria office and apartment tower. Or you can follow either of the two parallel passageways both of which lead to the Montreal Convention Centre.

The Jacques Parizeau Building (1000 Place Jean-Paul Riopelle), is a beautifully proportioned 2002 transparent glass building that has been described as a "horizontal skyscraper." It houses the Caisse de dépôt et placement du Québec which manages Quebec's pension funds. Designed by Gauthier, Daoust, and Lestage, the structure embraces three other buildings without overpowering them: the Hotel W., located in what was once the Bank of Canada building, the old *Montreal Herald* newspaper building, and a third building that dates from 1941. The main atrium, Le Parquet, is a 122-metre long alleyway of highly polished Brazilian ipe wood and a 42-metre high glass wall. It was the setting for the opening scenes of the 2011 Science fiction movie, *I Am Number Four*, starring Alex Pettyfer. Not only is the building a work of art, it houses works of art. At the east end of Le Parquet, hang two Quebec masterworks, Jean-Paul Riopelle's *Autriche,* and Rita Letendre's *Ode to Isis.* Scattered through the main floors are a Brazilian pine bas relief by André Genest, Michael Merrill's *Staircase*, and Jérôme Fortin's *Montage #1.* You will find Charles Daudelin's sculpture, *Femme Accroupe* and Geneviève Cadieux's *Serigraph June 2003* in a "secret" garden just off the building's main corridor. It's an ideal spot to sit in comparative seclusion. Also check out *Yama,* a contemplative lobby installation fashioned out of bamboo and stratified soil by award-winning artist Irene Whittome.

PHOTOS
1 The main atrium of the Jacques Parizeau Building
2 The "secret garden" just off the building's main corridor.

1 This unique sculpture-fountain, *La Joute* (The Joust), created by internationally-renowned painter and sculptor Jean-Paul Riopelle now resides in the square named after him. The fountain is encirled by a ring of fire, and is not to be missed. The city's convention hall is in the background.

2 Normand Laprise, the celebrated chef of the Toqué restaurant, situated on Place Jean-Paul Riopelle.

In the southeast corner you'll find the upscale restaurant, Toqué! (900 Jean-Paul Riopelle Place), considered by many to be among Canada's best. It owes its reputation to its chef, Normand Laprise, who changed the culinary vernacular by creating a unique Quebec gastronomy with locally sourced ingredients. Writing of Laprise, the *Canada's 100 Best Restaurants* website has this to say: "From Boileau venison to St-Canut suckling pigs, many of the products he helped nurture to market are now the mainstay of the best dining rooms across the country. Laprise likes them to star on his plates undisguised preferring instead to highlight their natural qualities with playful and unexpected contrasts of flavour and texture." The place has a corporate ambiance, and qualilty is expensive; a meal for two, not including wine, can be $300

Tour de la Bourse | Square Victoria

As you head south, there is a spur to your right that goes off to Square Victoria (created in 1860) and the Tour de la Bourse, otherwise known as the Stock Exchange Tower (800 Square-Victoria). Described by one architect as a "poem in concrete", the existing 190-metre high tower, which opened in 1965, is one of two originally designed by a master Italian engineer Pier Luigi Nervi (1891-1979). When the 48-storey building opened it was the largest reinforced concrete building in the world and Canada's tallest skyscraper. (*See photo opp. page*). The trading floor closed in 2001 when the exchange became fully automated and in 2007 it merged with the TSX group. There's not much to see except for the food courts and the chandelier that drops through the stairwell. A former hotel that was once part of the Stock Exchange complex has been converted into the EVO Student Residence Building. But gourmet chef Helena Loureiro's Portus 360 is a revolving restaurant on the 30th and 31st floor that offers breathtaking, panoramic views of the city.

The entrance to the Square-Victoria-OACI Metro station. The Art Nouveau entrance designed by Hector Guimard (1867-1942) was a gift of the Paris transit authority.

Centre de commerce mondiale (World Trade Centre)

Enter the World Trade Centre to discover the indoor city at its very best. The Trade Centre covers an entire block and contains retail and commercial space. When architect Ramesh Khosla conceived the plan in 1988 his challenge was to combine 17 different buildings on the site into a coherent whole that respects the integrity of the bits and pieces of the Victorian and Edwardian properties that had to be incorporated into the complex. Khosla came to Canada in 1965 to work with Arcop Architects in co-partnership on Place Bonaventure. He had been hired by Canadian financier Paul Desmarais Sr. to transform the old Canada Steamship Lines Building into the headquarters for Desmarais' Power Corporation. Around the same time he was asked to design the World Trade Centre. They were two separate projects. Although the Canada Steamship Lines building is at the west end of the World Trade Centre, Desmarais initially didn't want anything to do with the overall development plan. He was persuaded to change his mind when Aimé Desautels, who was with the City of Montreal's planning department, agreed to allow him to expropriate the service lane known as Rue des Fortifications which ran east and west through the block. "I wanted to bring as much daylight into the system as possible," Khosla explains, "the service lane allowed us to do that. It was the spine of the project, it was at street level, not underground." Desmarais had wanted a formal French garden incorporated into the scheme but Khosla argued that while such a garden could be built it would be difficult to maintain. He suggested, instead, a block-long black granite table fountain. His idea was accepted, and the granite was imported from India. "The result is a peaceful oasis, spacious and airy and bright, with the reflecting pool and an impressive statue of the sea goddess *Amphritite*, as its centerpiece. The work of the 18th century sculptor Dieudonné Barthelémy Guibal (1699-1757) it came from the town of Meuse in Northern France. The bricks that line the floor mark the footprint of the old Rue des Fortifications which is where the walls that once surrounded the old city once stood. "We broke new ground as far as the office environment is concerned," Khosla says, "People who have offices in the centre can open a door and step on to an interior balcony, giving you the feeling of being outdoors."

1 Sea goddess *Amphritite* by 18th century sculptor Dieudonné Barthelémy Guibal
2 The World Trade Centre atrium follows the route of the old
Ruelle de Fortifications.

At the far end of the passageway is a 2.5 tonne portion of the Berlin Wall, which was given to Montreal by the City of Berlin when Montreal observed its 350th anniversary in 1992. To the left is the 26-storey Intercontinental Hotel and the Sarah B. absinthe bar (named after actress Sarah Bernhardt). To the right, and up a flight of stairs, is the discreet entrance to the Nordheimer Block and the opulent Hotel Le St. James next door. The beautifully restored Nordheimer building was built in 1888 for the Nordheimer Piano Company. It is connected to the St. James Hotel, which was originally the Merchant Bank of Canada, and later the headquarters for the Nesbitt-Thompson brokerage firm. It was converted into a luxury boutique hotel that opened in 2002. The Rolling Stones once booked the entire building during a stopover in Montreal. Guests can also experience opulent dining in the XO restaurant, a plush room with sweeping staircases, glistening chandeliers and tables adorned with fine crystal and china. *Montreal Gazette* food critic Lesley Chesterman, recommends dinner at XO as "Luxury unparalleled in this city."

The doors to the left of the Berlin Wall open into the Hotel Intercontinental, also favoured by visiting rock stars and celebrities. Directly ahead are the doors to the 455-room Westin Hotel which was originally built as the head office for the Montreal *Star,* an English-language daily newspaper founded in 1869 that went out of business in 1979 following a ten-month strike. The Montreal *Gazette* then occupied the building for 20 years before it was converted into a hotel.

PHOTO
A fragment of the Berlin Wall.

Palais des congrès de Montréal / Montreal Convention Centre

In the hallway that links the Intercontinental and Westin hotels, the corridor to the left connects the World Trade Centre to the $200-million Palais des congrès. As you head down the stairs, you will pass a mural on your left, a montage of images created by Rafael Sottolichio to mark the trade centre's 20th anniversary. You are now in what is known as the St. Pierre Pathway, the last gap of the indoor pedestrian interchange to be completed. When it opened in 2003 it connected the World Trade centre to the Palais des congrès to create the world's largest indoor limited environment. The translucent photomontages on your right as you walk through the tunnel entitled *Sommeil (ou les sejours sous terre)* are by Isabelle Hayeur. Further along you'll see Michel Goulet's installation, *Tables*—stainless steel panels and a free standing steel chair. One of the panels has laser-cut flags of each of the 192 member countries in the United Nations.

Clad in imported Chinese granite, dressed in a psychedelic grid of yellow, green, pink and turquoise windows, and planted with Claude Cormier's playful forest of 52 lipstick-coloured concrete trees, the Palais des Congrès is one of the most visually animated spaces in the city. Cormier`s installation *Jardin légère / Lipstick Forest* is a winter garden inspired by the old stand of maple trees that once lined the avenue, and pays tribute to the city`s cosmetics industry. The wall of twinkling lights to your left as you arrive at the top of the escalator is the Constellation of Great Montrealers. It was inaugurated in 2012 to mark the 190th anniversary of the Board of Trade. Each year, the names of four deserving luminaries are inscribed in the wall of fame, which honours renowned Montrealers such as fromer Prime Minister Pierre Elliott Trudeau, hockey hero Jean Beliveau, playwright Michel Tremblay and architect and philanthropist Phyllis Lambert.

Running along one side of the vast indoor street is a 300-metre red-granite ribbon which commemorates all of the major trade shows and other events that have been held in the convention centre since it opened in 2002. One of the first pieces of public art to be installed in the convention centre is Micheline Beauchemin's aluminum mobile, *Nuages de soleil*, which is suspended in the convention centre's Viger lobby at the east end of the granite ribbon. The work, which is 11 metres long is made of 7,000 polished silver aluminum rods There is a rooftop where vegetables are grown, an urban agricultural project designed to improve air quality and provide fresh vegetables to the homeless.

The Place d' Armes Metro station is located at the east end of the convention centre.

Claude Cormier's "Lipstick Forest", Palais des Congrès

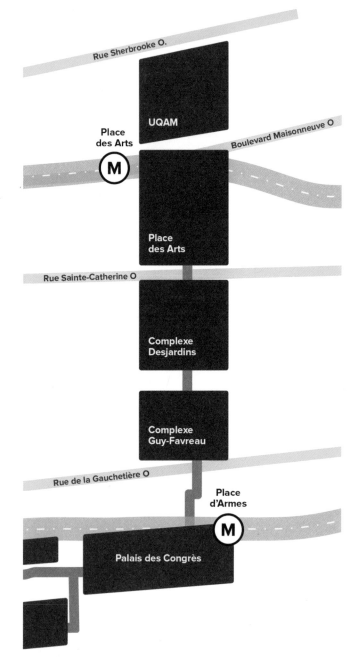

Quartier des spectacles

*"The underground city is not a **separate** city but a second city, that feeds and sustains the streets above…"*

– Adam Gopnick, the Massey Lectures

Complexe Guy-Favreau

Proceed through the underground tunnel that snakes into the next skyscraper. Or, if you prefer, go up the escalators and take a shortcut across the Chinese garden court outside which is especially beautiful in the spring when the cherry trees are in bloom. Either way, you will find yourself in Complexe Guy Favreau (200 René-Lévesque), a federal government complex in the heart of Montreal's Chinatown district. There are 316 apartment units in the complex; the mall below has been transformed into a Chinese community centre. The mall opens into an enormous atrium which is twelve stories high. Designed by Lemay, Dorval, Fortin and Doyle Architects, Complexe Guy Favreau opened in 1984, and it took another six years before it was plugged into the subterranean city. The building is named for a lawyer and jurist, Guy Favreau who was federal Justice Minister of Canada in the 1960s. There is a bronze bust of him on the mezzanine level by sculptor Raoul Hunter.

At the end of the atrium, turn left and take the steps down to the passageway that goes past the Post Office on your left, and you will find yourself in Complexe Desjardins.

PHOTOS
1 Sculpture, Complexe Place Guy-Favreau
2 Bronze bust of Guy Favreau by Raoul Hunter

GUY FAVREAU

Complexe Desjardins

Complexe Desjardins was originally conceived as a project to shift the city's centre of economic gravity from the English-speaking west end into the French speaking east-end of Montreal in 1970. Built by the Desjardins financial group, and designed by four different architects as a "people mecca," it was also meant to be an expression of confidence in the city which was shaken following the 1970 October Crisis in which a British trade commissioner was kidnapped and a Quebec cabinet minister was murdered. It took six years of wrangling and numerous construction delays and cost overruns before the $210-million complex opened in April, 1976, just in time for the XXI Olympic Games. The problem is the space, which covers 4.2-million square feet and needs large crowds of people to make it less intimidating. Planner and architect Mark London, writing in the Montreal *Star* several years after the four towers opened, pointed out that while Complexe Desjardins was the largest enclosed space of its type in the world, it was not a very coherent or successful shopping environment. It does however, house the only large grocery store in the underground city, the IGA. In the south west tower is the recently refurbished 600-room Hyatt Hotel, which is the perfect place to stay if you are in town in early late June/early July for the Montreal International Jazz Festival, which holds the Guinness World Record as the world's largest jazz festival. The enormous interior street which runs 65 metres between the towers was once Rue Benoit. It is 55 metres wide with a ceiling 28 metres above it.

PHOTOS
1 The spacious concourse in Complexe Desjardins
2 Montreal International Jazz Festival, Quartier des spectacles

Place des Arts

The tunnel linking Complexe Desjardins with Place des Arts cost $4-million to build and opened in 1977. Within the complex are four buildings—the main concert hall, a symphony hall, the Musée d'art contemporain, and three theatres. Walk through the tunnel until you slowly emerge into a labyrinth of wonder, the $12-Million Espace culturel Georges-Émile-Lapalme. Renovated in 2009, the hallway honours Lapalme, the Liberal cabinet minister who established Quebec's Cultural Affairs department in 1961, because as he stated, "The Americans will always be richer than us. They will always be able to dominate us. The same may be said of English Canada. Robbed of its culture, nothing will remain of French-Canada." The space is dominated by *Comme si le temps ... de la rue* a 1992 sculpture by Pierre Granche. It represents a stylized map of Montreal and is mounted with surreal aluminum figures, part bird, part human, adapted from Egyptian mythology. Veer off to the left, and you will be mesmerized by the ever changing mosaic on 35-video screen installations. Place des Arts itself, the multi-venue arts center complex, has six performance spaces, including a symphony hall, and a museum. Truly a crossroads for cultural life in the city, it is at the heart of a district known as the Quartier des Spectacles.

The inaugural concert in the multi-purpose 2,990-seat Salle Wilfrid-Pelletier concert hall took place in 1963 and was led by two eminent conductors, Wilfrid Pelletier and Zubin Mehta. There are two theatres along the east wall of the complex, the 1,500-seat Théatre Maisonneuve and the 800-seat Théatre Jean-Duceppe.

The west side of the arts complex houses the Musée d'art contemporain, (185 Sainte-Catherine W.) a showcase for modern art. There are more than 6,000 works in the collection, including artists such as Jean-Paul Riopelle, Paul-Émile Borduas and Geneviève Cadieux. Upstairs among the works in the sculpture court, is Henry Moore's *Upright Motive Number 5.* When the museum opened in 1992, they built another theatre, the Cinquième Salle. Depending on the configuration of the intimate hall, it can seat as few as 300 and as many

1 Tunnel passage, Place des arts.
2 *Comme si le temps...de la rue* sculpture by Pierre Granche

as 420. The theatre is equipped with a system of mobile platforms which can be adjusted to accommodate small groups or large scale performances.

The newest addition to the arts complex, **La Maison Symphonique** (1600 St. Urbain) a concert hall for the Montreal Symphony Orchestra, opened with a performance of Beethoven's Ninth Symphony in September, 2011. The 2,100-seat hall, off to the right, with its blond Quebec beechwood interior and Casavant Frères organ above the stage, is a spartan but functional space. Designed by Jack Diamond of Diamond & Schmitt, in collaboration with New York's Artec Consultants (who designed the acoustics), and the engineering firm SNC Lavalin, it's a rather egalatarian room: there are no segregated balconies.

If you want to grab a bite before the curtain rises on any of the performances in the building, Bistro Le Seingalt (1501 Jeanne Mance) to the left of the main doors of Place des Arts offers a distinctively French menu at reasonable prices. The name of the intimate bistro is of course Casanova's pseudonym. For an after theatre drink, the lobby wine bar, Deschamps (175 Sainte-Catherine W.), named for a revered Quebec comedian, Yvon Deschamps, is the ideal spot to relax. Continue to walk along the passage, past the Archambault music store on your right, until you come to the Place-des-Arts Metro station.

The east wall is graced with an iridescent stained glass mural illuminated with 105 neon tubes. Entitled *Les Arts lyriques*, it is an early work by Quebec artist, animator and Academy Award-winning filmmaker Frédéric Back (1924-2013). The installation was a gift from the now defunct Steinberg chain of grocery stores, and it depicts the evolution of music in Montreal, from the first trumpet fanfare to be sounded on the island on October 20, 1535, to the achievements of contemporary Quebec musicians, composers and conductors such as Calixa Lavallée, Emma Albani, Guillaume Couture and Alexis Contant.

The underground city is not exactly a mecca for discriminating music lovers, but buskers who regularly perform at designated locations within must audition in order to get a permit, so the musicians and street artists you encounter along the way are not without talent.

The tunnel curves into the sleek President Kennedy pavilion of the **Université du Québec** which opened in 1997 and houses the mathematics, science, and physics departments as well as a school of environmental studies. The building also contains the chemistry laboratories and is connected by a third floor skybridge to the Sherbrooke Pavilion, which began as a technical school in 1911. There is a giant mural by Montreal painter, dancer and sculptor Françoise Sullivan (1925 -) entitled *Montagnes.* Exit the building, and you will find yourself at 200 Sherbrooke Street, exactly ten blocks east of where you began.

Françoise Sullivan's mural, *Montagnes,* Université du Québec

The Future

There are now limits to Vincent de Pasciuto-Ponte's original vision of the multi-level city. He subscribed to a new form and as an architect, rather than cater to his client's presumed intentions, managed to create something far more innovative than what his clients had in mind. Although the first loop is finished, there is no limit to the imagination of how Montreal's underground city will grow, and what new avenues may plug into the network. The latest addition is the super hospital which can be accessed through the Champ-de-Mars Metro station. The next phase could conceivably see the new Griffintown development south of the Bell Centre, the expanded Montreal Museum of Fine Arts and the Concordia University campus plugged into the system.

It is easy to trivialize the impact of the climate controlled city. One fatuous commentator on CBC radio recently complained that "the underground city sucks," that it was nothing more than a collection of shopping malls. But landscape architect Ron Williams points out that when it was built, it was "totally original, and was better than anything in the world. Montreal is the absolute leader in terms of urban and environmental design, and the inspiration for what is happening in Tokyo."

Admittedly the challenge now is to create a feeling of warmth in the endless passageways and devise a transition that not only mirrors what is above ground but one that adds a certain cachet to key features that are indoors. "It could continue to expand, but with great difficulty," says architect Ramesh Khosla, "If it was to be really underground, it would be very confined, and not considered desirable. A lot of the original passages which are underground are really now derelict. You will have to find much more imaginative ways to link the buildings together."

As architect Avi Friedman points out, the underground experience has to be much more than a series of tunnels connecting high rises. "The passage ways are not there only for the convenience of pedestrians, but for economic reasons. There has to be an economic component. If there are no shops or nothing attractive in the passageways it makes it difficult and expensive to expand the network. There is also the legal issue: If there are long stretches of empty tunnels who is liable for any accident that happens in them if there is no source of revenue or insurance."

In 2007 three teams of international landscape architects from Montreal, Brazil and Germany, took part in a UNESCO sponsored workshop and reimagined the design of Place d'Armes, one of Old Montreal's most historic squares. Drawing on plans which once included the courthouse and city hall as part of the network, designers came up with an imaginative three-tier development, featuring illuminated rooms and narrative trails linking the Place d'Armes Metro station and the Palais des congrès with Notre-Dame Basilica. The idea is not new. It was first proposed in the 1960s but was abandoned as being too costly. Should it prove to be practical down the road, the sunken park, underground galleries and a system of reflecting pools, would highlight the footprints of the original parish church which stood in the middle of the square for almost 70 years until it was torn down in the 1830s. It is but one of a plethora of ideas that will undoubtedly shape the future of the sheltered city.

Metro signage ranging from the 1960's to the 2000's.

Getting Around – Useful Information

INFO TOURIST CENTRE
Information on Montreal and other Quebec destinations
1255 Peel Street, Suite 100
Metro Peel (corner of Sainte-Catherine Street West)

Phone: Montréal area: 514-844-5400
Toll free, from Canada and U.S.A.: 1-800 230-0001
E-mail: info@mtl.org
Fax: 514-844-5757

BUS AND MÉTRO - Société de transport de Montréal (STM)
Regular fare: $3.25
Reduced fare: age 6 -11
Where to purchase: On the bus with the exact change
In the metro from a ticket booth attendant

2-Trip fare: $6
Can be used for 120 minutes once it has been validated
In the metro from a ticket booth attendant or at one of the STM's
points of sale

3-Day fare: $18
Unlimited travel for three consecutive days from the time it is validated.
This fare is valid on the P.-E. Trudeau/Downtown shuttle (#747).
Where to purchase: In the métro from a fare vending machine, a fare
booth attendant, or at one of the STM's points of sale.

Pierre-Elliot Trudeau 747 Airport Bus
$10 for everyone. Free for children aged 5 and under at all times.
Can be paid in cash with exact change on board the bus. Only coins are
accepted (no bank bills. A 24-hour service, that includes 11 stops.
Phone: 514-786-4636 | stm.info/747

PASSEPORT MONTRÉAL
48-hour pass $85+ tax
72-hour pass $99 + tax

Passeport MTL includes the price of admission for one adult (18 years and older) to a total of 23 major city attractions (museums, the Insectarium, Botanical Garden etc.). Unlimited public transportation.

PIERRE-ELLIOTT TRUDEAU INTERNATIONAL AIRPORT
Phone: 514-394-7377
admtl.com

MONTREAL CENTRAL TRAIN STATION – Gare centrale
895 Rue de la Gauchetière O, Montréal, QC H3B 4G1
Phone: 1- 888-842-7245 | 514-898-2626

MONTREAL BUS TERMINAL - Gare d'autocars de Montréal
Departure and arrival point for most inter-city buses
1717 Berri Street
Phone: (514) 842-2281

MEGABUS
Low cost bus service
997 St-Antoine Ouest (Métro Bonaventure)
Phone: 1- 866-488-4452
megabus.com

TAXIS
Can be hailed, found at a taxi stand, or called directly. At the time of writing Uber is still operating in Montreal

BIKING
Bixi
Phone: 514-789-2494
montreal.bixi.com
You can borrow a bike (April to November) from one station and re-dock the bike at another station.

Photo Credits

19 Alan Hustak; 21 Alan Hustak; 23 (top) Alan Hustak, (bottom) Simon Dardick; 25 (top) Andre Atilin/Creative Commons, (bottom) Ancien et modern/Creative Commons; 27 Jean Gagnon/Creative Commons; 29 Jean Gagnon/Creative Commons; 33 Guilhem Vellut/Creative Commons; 34 Simon Dardick; 37 Alan Hustak; 39 Alan Hustak; 41 (top) Andrevuas/Creative Commons, (bottom) Alan Hustak; 43 Alan Hustak; 47 Alan Hustak; 49 Jean-Michel Crettaz and Mark-David Hosale/Creative Commons; 50 Alan Hustak; 52 (top) Alan Hustak, (bottom) ©Benedicte Brocard/Creative Commons https://creativecommons.org/licenses/by-sa/4.0/deed.en; 54 Jean Gagnon/Creative Commons; 55 LogosV/Creative Commons; 57 Alan Hustak; 59 Jean Gagnon/Creative Commons; 61 Alan Hustak; 65 Alan Hustak; 67 (top) Alan Hustak, (bottom) Matias Garabedian/Creative Commons; 69 Alan Hustak; 71 Jean Gagnon/Creative Commons; 75 Société de transport de Montréal; 76 Courtesy of Matt Soar, Montreal Signs Project Collection, Concordia University (donation from the Société de transport de Montréal).

*Where an image has been used under a licence through Creative Commons, the licence can be found at: https://creativecommons.org/licenses/by-sa/2.5/legalcode

Index

Alan Hustak is a veteran journalist who has written about all things Montreal. He is the author of several books, including *Titanic: The Canadian Story*; and *Faith Under Fire: Frederick Scott, Canada's Extraordinary Chaplain of the Great War*. He divides his time between Montreal, Quebec and Fort Qu'Appelle, Saskatchewan.